Dedicated to the life and memory of my beloved
grandparents, Dan and Ann Freedman,
who gave me tons of laughter.

You Are My Sunshine

My mother, Barbara Duran, is the inspiration for Aunt Buttercream.
Her silliness makes every day a fun day for learning.
Thank you, Mom, for being you.
Mrs. Flutterbee is my alter ego. Like her, even when I'm afraid,
I have silly fun trying new things.

Kati Bee And Friends, Publishing
Riverside, California
www.katibeeandfriends.com

©2007 Kati Bee and Friends. Mrs. Flutterbee and the Kati Bee and Friends logo are trademarks of Kati Bee and Friends. All rights reserved. Unauthorized duplication prohibited by federal law.

Book design and paintings by Hugh Dunnahoe.
Printed in Korea.

Bee, Kati.
Mrs. Flutterbee and the funny farm / by Kati Bee;
illustrated by Hugh Dunnahoe.
p. cm.
SUMMARY: A teacher, silly Mrs. Flutterbee, visits a farm with her class.
She overcomes her fear of the animals with the help of a secret friend.
Audience: Ages 3-8.
LCCN 2007924519
ISBN-13: 978-0-9793760-0-9
ISBN-10: 0-9793760-0-9
1. Fear–Juvenile fiction. 2. Domestic animals–Juvenile fiction.
3. School field trips–Juvenile fiction. [1. Fear–Fiction. 2. Farm life–Fiction.
3. Animals–Fiction.]   I. Dunnahoe, Hugh, ill. II. Title.

PZ7.B381965Mrs 2007
[E]
QBI07-600146

Mrs. Flutterbee and the Funny Farm

by Kati Bee

Illustrated by Hugh Dunnahoe

Mrs. Flutterbee is a very silly teacher. She took her class to visit a farm. It was not like any other farm. It was Aunt Buttercream's farm, and she is almost as silly as Mrs. Flutterbee.

Buzz, Mrs. Flutterbee's secret friend, came too.

"Howdy!" said Aunt Buttercream. "Welcome to my funny farm. Breakfast is served, so dig in!"

Mrs. Flutterbee giggled. The class giggled. They never had dessert for breakfast before.

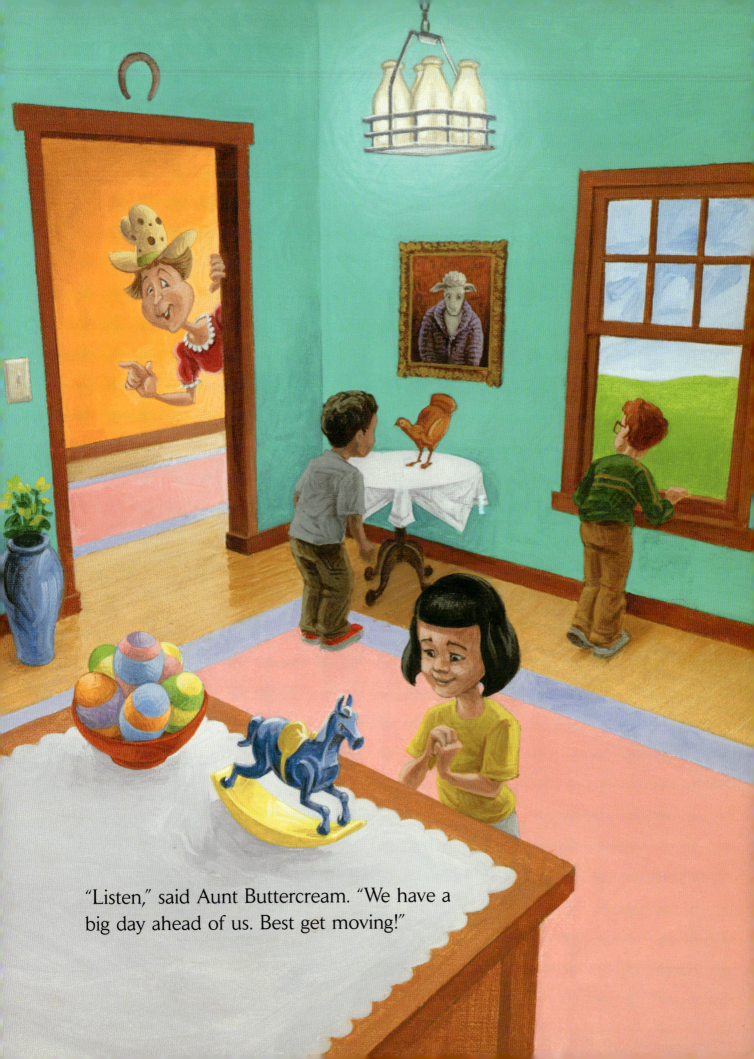

"Listen," said Aunt Buttercream. "We have a big day ahead of us. Best get moving!"

"First, we will visit my friend in the barn. Skip to it!" said Aunt Buttercream. Skipping away, she sang,

"One, two, three – follow me. Lots to do and lots to see."

Aunt Buttercream skipped into the barn and the children followed. Mrs. Flutterbee stopped. She saw two pointy horns and heard a low voice moaning.

"Moo! Moo! Moo–oo!"

"It's The Beast With Horns!" cried Mrs. Flutterbee, running away—hat flopping and shoes bopping.

"Oh no!" said Buzz. He knew Mrs. Flutterbee would need his help because she is afraid of new things. "Do not be afraid," he whispered. "That's not The Beast With Horns. She is our new friend."

Aunt Buttercream spun around and sang a riddle.

"Tell me now, what do I see? What does it do for you and me?"

"It's not The Beast With Horns," giggled Mrs. Flutterbee. "Is it for scaring the mice away?"

The children shouted, "She's a cow and she gives us milk!"

"That's right," said Aunt Buttercream. She then showed everyone how to milk the cow.

It sure looked easy when
Aunt Buttercream did it.

"It's time to visit my friend at the stable," said Aunt Buttercream. "Hop to it!" Hopping like a bunny, she sang,

"One, two, three – follow me. Lots to do and lots to see."

Singing along, Mrs. Flutterbee and her class followed, hopping like bunnies.

Aunt Buttercream and the class hopped to the stable. Mrs. Flutterbee saw a tail waving in the air behind a haystack. She heard a strange sound.

"Neigh! Neigh! Neigh!"

She jumped—hat flopping and shoes bopping. "It's Big Foot the Hairy Monster!" she screamed.

"Do not be afraid," said Buzz, "I'm right here. He is not Big Foot the Hairy Monster. He is our friend."

Aunt Buttercream clapped her hands and sang,

"What is this? What could it be? How is it good for you and me?"

"I know he's not a hairy monster," giggled Mrs. Flutterbee. "Does he wash the dishes?"

The children laughed, "He's a horse and he gives us rides!"

"Right again," said Aunt Buttercream. She then showed everyone how to ride the horse.

It sure looked easy when Aunt Buttercream did it.

Aunt Buttercream had even more fun to share. "Hurry kids, stay close behind. We're off to the meadow." Waddling like a duck, she sang,

"One, two, three – follow me. Lots to do and lots to see."

Aunt Buttercream and the class waddled all the way to the middle of the meadow. Mrs. Flutterbee looked around. She saw white fluffy clouds lying in the tall grass, and they were making sounds!

"Baa! Baa! Baa–a–a!"

Mrs. Flutterbee yelled, "The sky is falling! The sky is falling!"

Aunt Buttercream bounced and sang,

"What are these? What do we see?
How do they help both you and me?"

"I thought they were fluffy clouds, but now I see they are not," sighed Mrs. Flutterbee.

The children shouted, "They are sheep, and they give us wool!"

"Very good," said Aunt Buttercream. She then showed everyone how to shear wool from the sheep.

It sure looked easy when Aunt Buttercream did it.

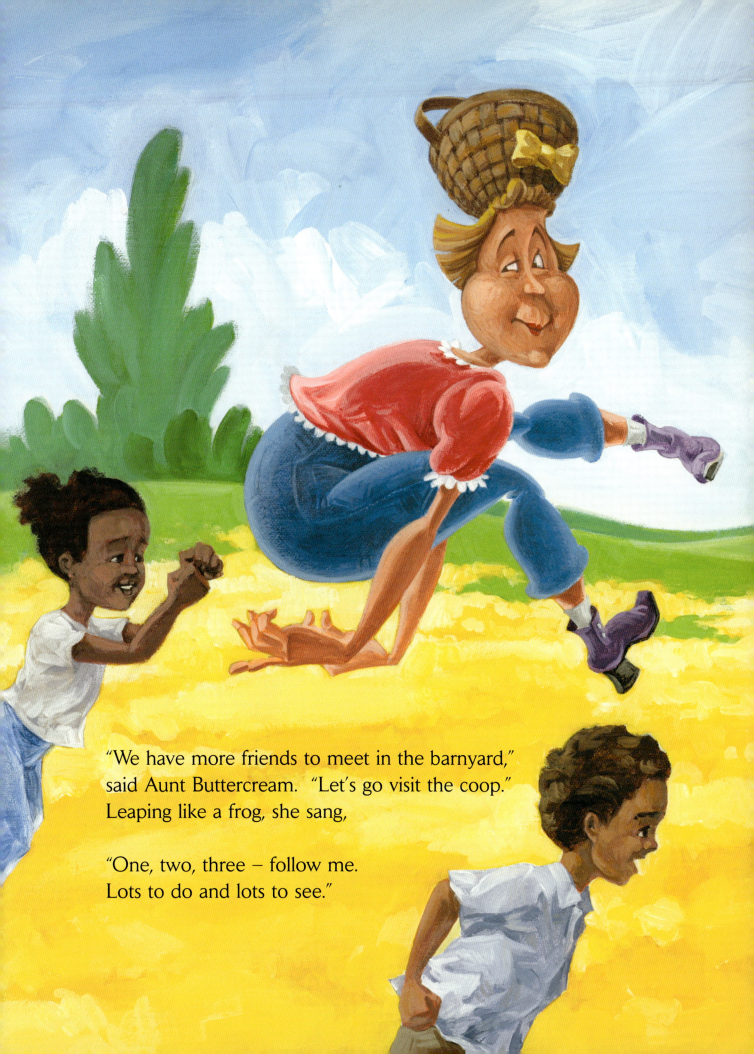

"We have more friends to meet in the barnyard," said Aunt Buttercream. "Let's go visit the coop." Leaping like a frog, she sang,

"One, two, three – follow me.
Lots to do and lots to see."

Everyone leaped and leaped and leaped all the way to the coop. Mrs. Flutterbee was so tired that she wanted to rest. She saw two feathery pillows, and tried to sit down.

"Cluck, cluck, cluck!"
"Cock-a-doodle-do!"

Mrs. Flutterbee jumped. She jumped so high she landed in a tree—hat flopping and shoes bopping.

"Don't be afraid!" said Buzz. "Come and meet our feathered friends."

Aunt Buttercream laughed and sang a new riddle,

"What are these that we have found? Why do we keep them all around?"

Mrs. Flutterbee said, "They're certainly not pillows!"

The children answered, "They are hens, and they give us eggs."

"The rooster wakes everyone up in the morning," said one little boy.

"Wonderful!" said Aunt Buttercream. "Let's gather eggs for our lunch."

Mrs. Flutterbee giggled. The class giggled.
They never had breakfast for lunch before.

Everyone thanked Aunt Buttercream for the fun day at the farm. "Thank you for our new friends," they said.

"Thank you, Buzz," whispered Mrs. Flutterbee, "for helping me today."

They waved goodbye and then skipped, hopped, waddled, and leaped onto the bus, singing,

"One, two, three – follow me. Lots to do and lots to see!"